MILITARY MACHINES
At Work

Military Trucks

By E. S. Budd

The Child's World®, Inc.

Published by The Child's World®, Inc.
PO Box 326
Chanhassen, MN 55317-0326
800-599-READ
www.childsworld.com

Design and Production:
The Creative Spark, San Juan Capistrano, CA

Photos: © 2002 David M. Budd Photography

We thank the personnel at Fort Carson (Colorado Springs, CO)
for their help and cooperation in preparing this book.

Library of Congress Cataloging-in-Publication Data

Budd, E. S.
Military trucks / by E.S. Budd.
        p. cm.
ISBN 1-56766-982-4 (Library bound : alk. paper)
1. Military trucks—Juvenile literature.
[1. Military trucks. 2. Trucks.]   I. Title.
UG615 .B83 2001
623.7'47—dc21
                                2001000339

Contents

On the Job

On the job, military trucks take soldiers where they want to go.

The military uses trucks for many things. Sometimes trucks are used to carry **troops.** The troops sit in the back. A truck can also carry **cargo** and **equipment.**

Military trucks have powerful **engines.**

Sometimes a military truck must
travel through deep water. Its engine
needs air to run. A special pipe gets
air to the engine even if most of the
truck is underwater.

The engine is underneath the **cab.**

Sometimes the engine needs to be fixed.

The soldier uses **controls** to tip the cab

forward. Then he can reach the engine.

Military trucks have big, tough tires.

The trucks can travel over rough ground.

They can also go up and down steep hills.

Some military trucks have special equipment to tow other **vehicles.** They can pull a tank out of a ditch. They can also tow vehicles that need to be fixed.

Military trucks have headlights.

They also have a blackout light. This special light helps soldiers travel at night without being seen. The blackout light is not as bright as the headlights. It has a cover. It aims the light at the ground.

TIE-DOWN

Climb Aboard!

Would you like to see where the driver sits? The military truck has a steering wheel, just like a car. The driver uses controls to drive the truck. Mirrors help the driver see all around.

Up Close

The inside

1. The steering wheel

2. The controls

3. The troop and cargo area

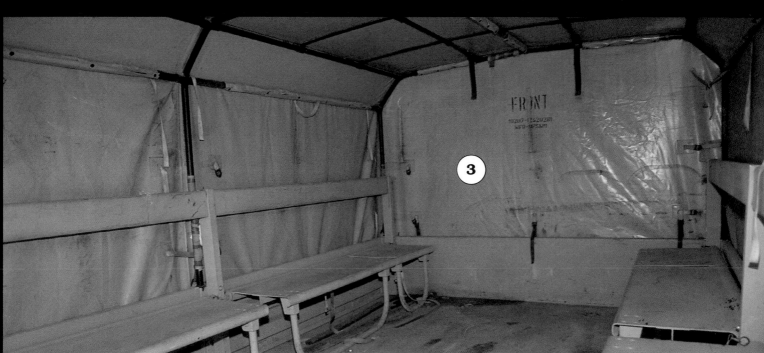

The outside

1. The lights

2. The blackout light

3. The cab

4. The mirror

5. The tires

6. The troop and cargo area

Glossary

cab (KAB)
A cab is the place where a driver sits. A military truck has a cab.

cargo (KAR-goh)
Cargo is a load of goods carried by a vehicle. A military truck can carry cargo.

controls (kun-TROHLZ)
Controls are buttons, switches, and other tools that make a machine work. A driver uses controls to drive a military truck.

engines (EN-jenz)
Engines are motors that use energy to make machines move or run. A military truck has a powerful engine.

equipment (ee-KWIP-ment)
Equipment is the tools that are needed for doing something. A military truck can carry equipment.

troops (TROOPZ)
Troops are soldiers. A military truck can carry troops from place to place.

vehicles (VEE-hih-kulz)
Vehicles are machines that take people or things from one place to another. A military truck is a vehicle.